To

....

From

....

To Sharon J.W.

Compiled by Lois Rock
Illustrations copyright © 2000 John Wallace
This edition copyright © 2000 Lion Publishing

The moral rights of the author and illustrator
have been asserted

Published by
Lion Publishing plc
Sandy Lane West, Oxford, England
www.lion-publishing.co.uk
ISBN 0 7459 4449 3
Lion Publishing
4050 Lee Vance View, Colorado Springs,
CO 80918, USA
ISBN 0 7459 4449 3

First UK edition 2000
10 9 8 7 6 5 4 3 2 1 0
First US edition 2001
10 9 8 7 6 5 4 3 2 1

A catalogue record for this book is available
from the British Library

Library of Congress CIP data applied for

Typeset in 14/21 Latin 725 BT
Printed and bound in Singapore

Acknowledgments
Thanks go to all those who have given permission
to include poems in this book, as indicated in
the list below. Every effort has been made to
trace and contact copyright owners. If there
are any inadvertent omissions or errors in the
acknowledgments, we apologize to those concerned
and will remedy these in the next edition.

'How far is it to Bethlehem?' by
Frances Chesterton from *The Oxford
Book of Carols,* reproduced by permission
of Oxford University Press.

'Donkey plod and Mary ride' by
Timothy Dudley-Smith, copyright
© Timothy Dudley-Smith, used by
permission.

'Think of a gift', 'It's Christmas time' by
Lois Rock, copyright © Lion Publishing plc.

Christmas
Rhymes & carols

compiled by Lois Rock
Illustrated by John Wallace

LION
Children's Books

Now light one thousand Christmas lights
On dark earth here tonight;
One thousand, thousand also shine
To make the dark sky bright.

Traditional Swedish

Donkey plod and Mary ride,
weary Joseph walk beside,
theirs the way that all men come,
dark the night and far from home—

down the years remember them,
come away to Bethlehem.

Timothy Dudley-Smith

How far is it to Bethlehem?
Not very far.
Shall we find the stable-room
Lit by a star?

Can we see the little child,
Is he within?
If we lift the wooden latch
May we go in?

Frances Chesterton (died 1938)

Away in a manger, no crib for a bed,
The little Lord Jesus laid down his
 sweet head.
The stars in the bright sky looked
 down where he lay,
The little Lord Jesus asleep on the hay.

Anonymous

Ox and ass at Bethlehem
On a night ye know of them;
We were only creatures small
Hid by shadows on the wall.

We were swallow, moth and mouse;
The Child was born in our house,
And the bright eyes of us three
Peeped at His Nativity.

Bruce Blunt

Silent night, holy night,
All is calm, all is bright
Round yon virgin mother and child;
Holy infant so tender and mild,
Sleep in heavenly peace,
Sleep in heavenly peace.

Joseph Mohr (1792–1848)
Translation: Anonymous

An azure sky,
All star bestrewn.
A lowly crib,
A hushèd room.
An open door,
A hill afar,
Where little lambs
And shepherds are.
To such a world,
On such a night,
Came Jesus—
Little Lord of Light.

Mary I. Osborn

Think of a gift for a baby boy:
A cuddly quilt and a special toy.

Think of a gift for a baby king:
All that the rich and the wise can bring.

Think of a gift for the baby you love:
All the blessings of God above.

What can I give Him,
Poor as I am?
If were a shepherd
I would bring a lamb,
If I were a Wise Man
I would do my part,—
Yet what I can I give Him,
Give my heart.

Christina Rossetti (1830–94)

It's Christmas time,
When angels come
To earth from heaven above.
Take a golden gift box
And fill it full of love.

It's Christmas time!
The angels' song
Is heard upon the ground.
Open up the gift box,
Let love shine all around.

Somehow, not only for Christmas
But all the long year through,
The joy you give to others
Is the joy that comes back to you.

John Greenleaf Whittier (1807–92)

We wish you a merry Christmas,
We wish you a merry Christmas,
We wish you a merry Christmas
And a happy New Year.

Good tidings we bring
To you and your kin;
We wish you a merry Christmas
And a happy New Year.

Traditional English